This book belongs to

....

Dance
party

by Mary Atkinson

make
believe
ideas

Get the most from this reader

Before reading:

Look at the pictures and discuss them together. Ask questions such as, "What shape are the crab's glasses?"

Relate the topic to your child's world. For example, say: "Did you enjoy dancing at Grandpa's party?"

Familiarise your child with book vocabulary by using terms such as *word*, *letter*, *title*, *author* and *text*.

During reading:

Prompt your child to sound out unknown words. Draw attention to neglected middle or end sounds.

Encourage your child to use the pictures as clues to unknown words.

Occasionally ask what might happen next, and then check together as you read on.

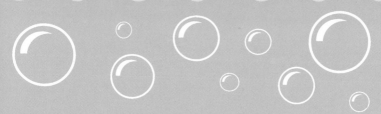

- Monitor your child's understanding. Repeated readings can improve fluency and comprehension.

- Keep reading sessions short and enjoyable. Stop if your child becomes tired or frustrated.

• •

After reading:

- Discuss the book. Encourage your child to form opinions with questions such as, "What did you like best about this book?"

- Help your child work through the fun activities at the back of the book. Then ask him or her to reread the story. Praise any improvement.

The fish had a party under the sea.

"Who wants to dance?"
said Chris the crab.

"I want to dance," said Betty the blue fish. "Here I come!"

"I want to dance,"
said Pete the purple fish.
"Watch me wiggle!"

"I want to dance,"
said Yan the yellow fish.
"Let's make some noise."

"I want to dance,"
said Olivia the orange fish.
"Let's have some fun."

"I don't want to dance," said Shay the shark.

Discussion Questions

1. What colour is the fish called Greg?

2. Why do the fish run away from Shay the shark?

3. Would you like to go to this party? Why?

❧ Sight Words ❧

Learning sight words helps you read fluently. Practise these sight words from the book. Use them in sentences of your own.

make

look

some

said

who

under

want

let

Snacks

♋ Rhyming Words ♋

Can you find the rhyming pairs?
Say them aloud.

my had to

by

do

bad

Writing Practice

Read the words, and then trace
them with your finger.

want

here

come

look

have

under

❧ Silly Sentences ❧

Have fun filling in the gap in each sentence. Use the ideas below or make up your own.

I don't want to ....

I want to ....